Dedicated to

Lara, Garrett, Devin and Buddy
Always know YOU are my favorite!

I love you!

AM I YOUR FAVORITE?

Written by
Gretchen Kadillak

Illustrated by
Susan Crum

My **dream** of being a **mom** came true,

when one by one

I welcomed **you!**

My babies, you **grew,**

you learned to **walk,**

and pretty soon
began to **talk.**

First came one word, then two... three... four...

then five... six... seven... and even more.

YES RUN
WALK
DOG UP
FUN HI CAT
DOWN DAD BYE
TALK
MOM NO

And then with all the **words** you knew,
came questions like,

"Mom, how old
are you?"

"Mom, tell me why
the sky is blue?"

Your love of questions
continued to grow...

"Am I your favorite?"

you wanted to know.

And this is the silly game we'd play:

"Who's my favorite?" I'd ask each day.

Is it the **one** who found our favorite puppy...

Is it the one who loves the color pink...

...and very **proudly** learned to **wink?**

As I try to

decide,

I will have to **think...**

...and always gives

the biggest hugs?

Or visits koalas
at the zoo...

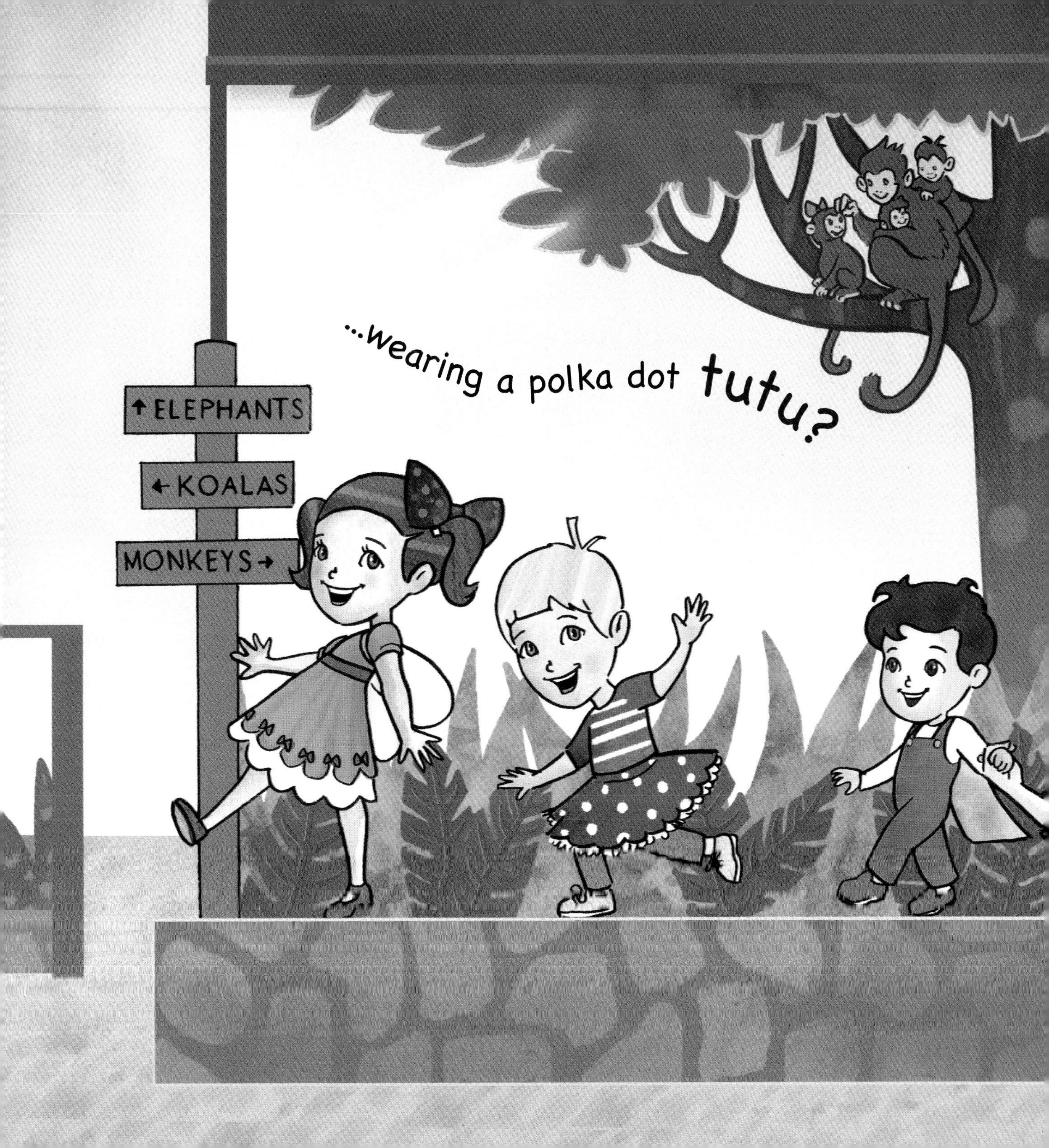

...wearing a polka dot **tutu?**

Who IS my favorite?

Is it the one who **makes** a paper rocket...

...with **secret** treasures in every pocket?

Is it the **one** who loves a **high**, **high** toss...

...or the one who **loves** noodles with **no sauce?**

So WHO is my favorite?

I'll tell you WHO...

It is each and
every one of
you!

I adore the way you
laugh and play,

and the way you
love me every day!

Always know that **I love YOU!**

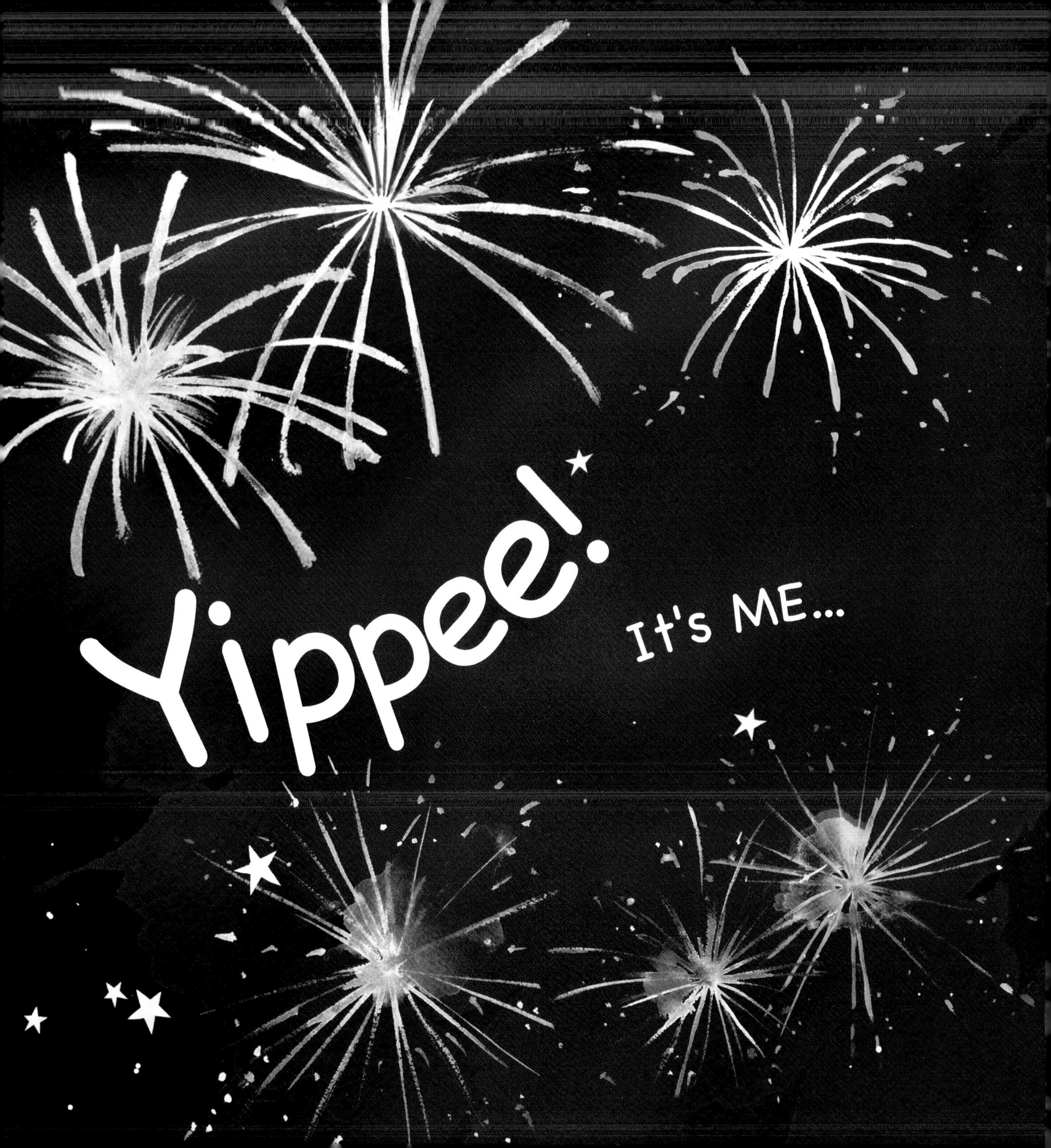

Yippee!

It's ME...

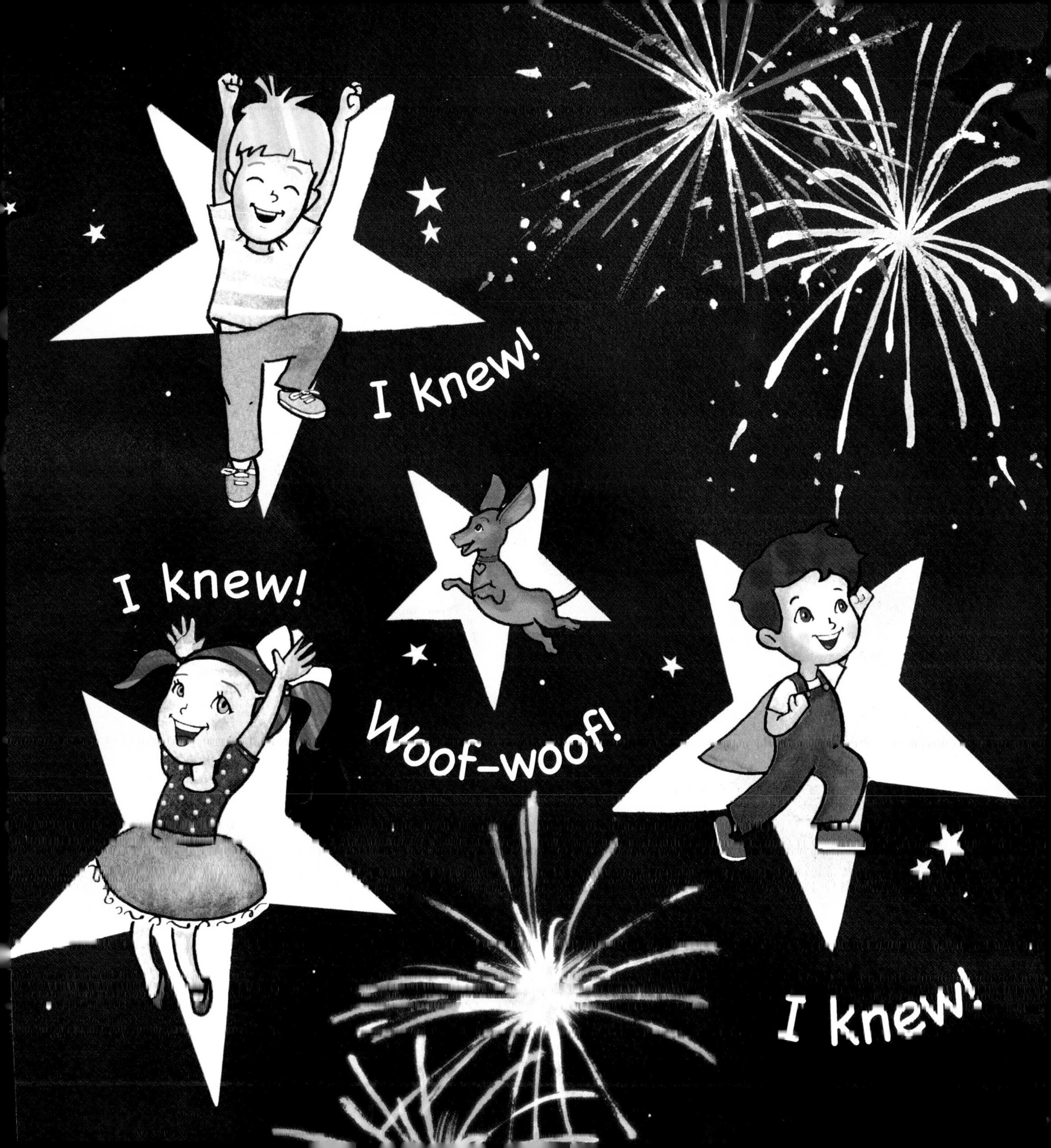
I knew!
I knew!
Woof-woof!
I knew!

How did you like the book?
We would love to have your feedback and
review on Amazon or Goodreads.

Download your FREE bonus content from
apowerfulyou.com.

GRETCHEN KADILLAK

Author

Gretchen Kadillak is a Life Coach and owner of A Powerful You, a company that provides life coaching that specializes in self-care. As part of her own self-care, Gretchen has written this book as a love letter to her three children, who are now grown. Remembering the special times they shared reading bedtime stories is what inspired Gretchen to create this legacy project. Her future writing plans include more children's stories and a self-care workbook. Gretchen and her husband live in Colorado.

Visit Gretchen's website to find out more about her offerings:

www.apowerfulyou.com

Illustrator

SUSAN CRUM

is an illustrator and chalk artist from Winnipeg, Canada. She now lives in Colorado with her husband and two children.

A special thank you for making my dream a reality...so grateful for:

My husband, Mike, for always being there and supporting me
every step of the way. Love you!

My illustrator, Susan, for all your creativity, insight
and talent to truly bring the book to life.

My dream team, April Cox, Praise Saflor, Bobbi Hinman,
for all your support, advice and encouragement.

All my family and friends that believed in me and were the best cheerleaders.

Thank you all for lifting me up through the breakdowns
and celebrating my breakthroughs!

Am I Your Favorite?

Published by A Powerful You, LLC
www.apowerfulyou.com
Copyright © 2021 Gretchen Kadillak

Text design and layout: Praise Saflor

Library of Congress Control Number: 2021934986

Publisher's Cataloging-in-Publication data

Names: Kadillak, Gretchen, author. | Crum, Susan, illustrator.
Title: Am I your favorite? / written by Gretchen Kadillak; illustrated by Susan Crum.
Description: Aurora, CO: A Powerful You, 2021. | Summary: A children's mother plays a game
with her children, letting them guess her favorite by sharing her favorite things about each.
Identifiers: LCCN: 2021934986 | ISBN: 978-1-7367691-1-9 (hardcover) | 978-1-7367691-0-2 (paperback) |
978-1-7367691-2-6 (ebook) | 978 1 7367691 3 3 (audio)
Subjects: LCGH Mother and child Juvenile fiction. | Family Juvenile fiction. | CYAC Mother
and child Fiction. | Family Fiction. | BISAC JUVENILE FICTION / Family / General |
JUVENILE FICTION / Family / Siblings | JUVENILE FICTION / Social Themes / Emotions & Feelings
Classification: LCC PZ7.1.K16 Am 2021 | DDC [E]--dc23